Meet the Helpers

CONTENTS

NATIONAL GEOGRAPHIC School Publishing
Hampton-Brown

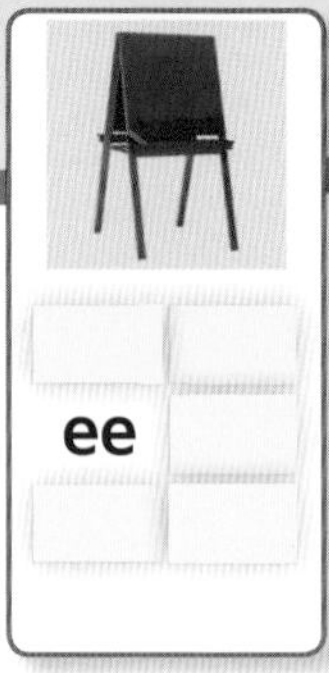

Words with **ee**

Look at each picture. Read the words.

Example:

qu**ee**n

b**ee**

tr**ee**

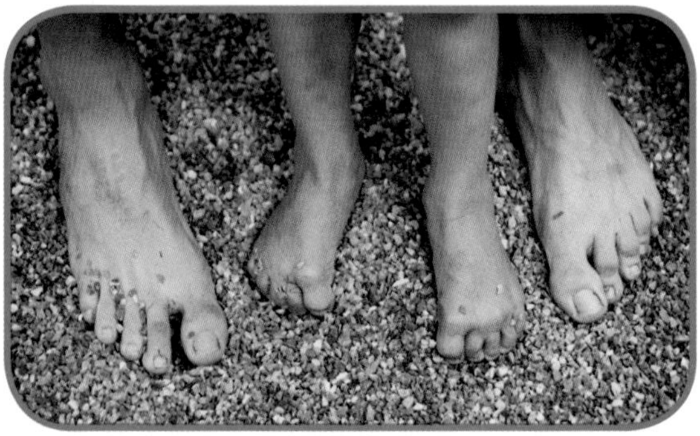

f**ee**t

cr**ee**k

fift**ee**n

High Frequency
Words

- been
- both
- different
- friend
- great
- house
- kind
- place

Key Words

Look at the picture. Read the sentences.

Best Friends

1. This is a **great** **place** to have lunch with a **friend**.
2. Each kid has a **different** **kind** of lunch.
3. Sam made lunch at his **house**.
4. **Both** friends have **been** in line for a time.

What Kind of lunch do you have?

GO! **Phonics Games**
NGReach.com

The Good Deeds Day

by Kate Pershing
illustrated by Valeria Cis

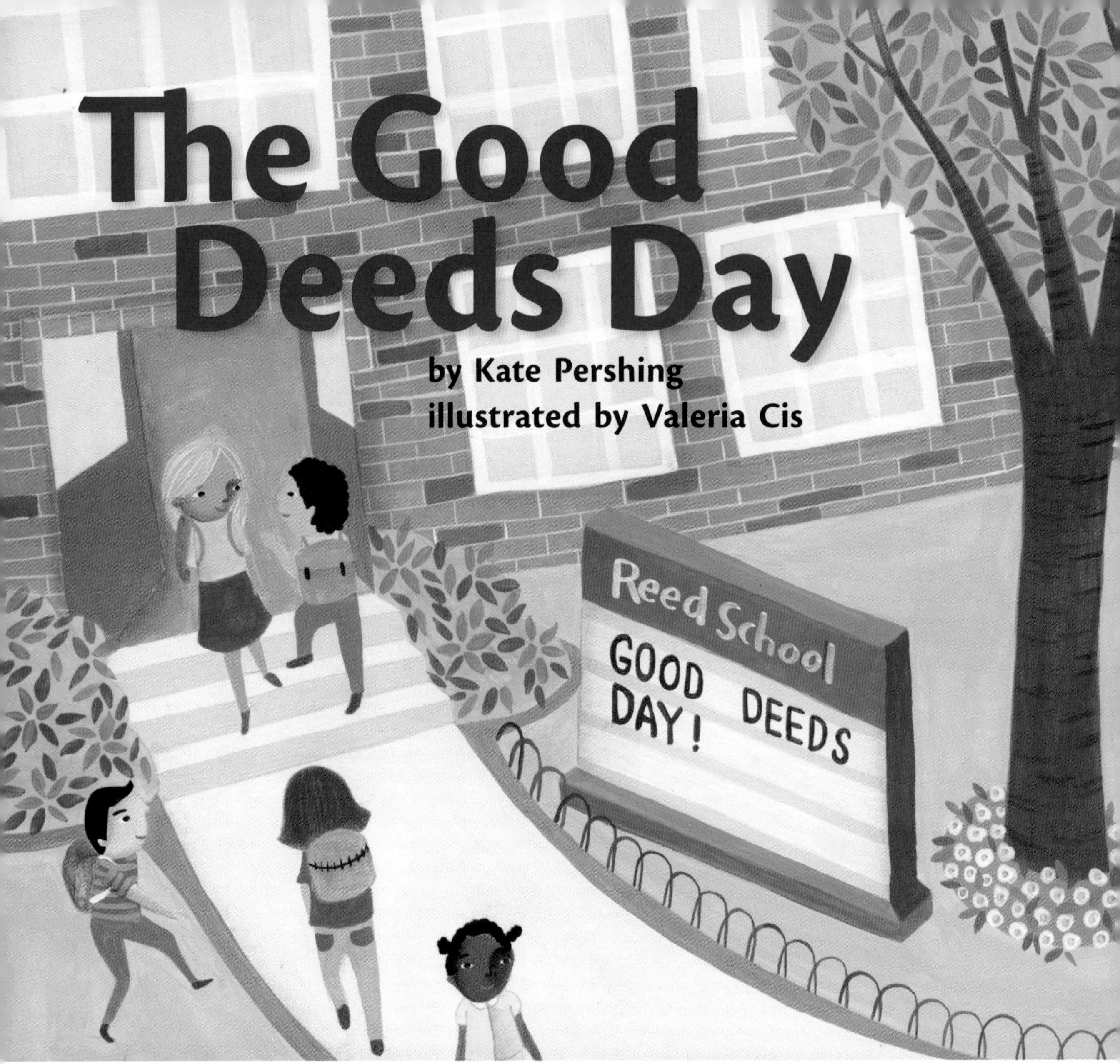

Our school has a Good Deeds Day. We give a prize to people who do good deeds for us. Who will get the prize? Think about these helpers at school.

We ride the bus to school. We need to feel safe on our ride. It is great to have this helper at the wheel. She is kind to us.

We need help to cross the street. This man stops traffic for us. We can go when we see the green light.

This dog helps a boy cross the street. This is a different kind of helper. It is a Helper Dog. The boy cannot see well. His dog helps him get from place to place.

If you have a pain or get a bee sting, you'll need to go here for help. The nurse can help you feel better.

When it's time for lunch, these people feed us. We line up and they greet us with a big smile.

This man has an important job. When we go home, he sweeps away the dust under the desks.

If you need to call your house, here is someone who can help. It may seem that she has a lot to do, but she will be free in a bit. Then she'll call your mom or dad for you.

This helper gets us the books we need. If we needed a book about deer or bees, he'd help us get it.

This is the best helper. She helps us to do math and spelling. We like her and she feels the same about us.

We've got lots of helpers. Who will get the Good Deeds prize? Ask a friend. You may agree that it is hard to pick just one person. Let's give a prize to all of them!

Words with **ee**

Read these words.

three	fifteen	plant	creek	picnic
weed	screen	seedlings	swim	sweep

Find the words with **ee**.
Use letters to build them.

t h r e e

Talk Together

Choose words from the box above to tell your partner how children can help do good deeds at home and at school.

They can help sweep.

1.

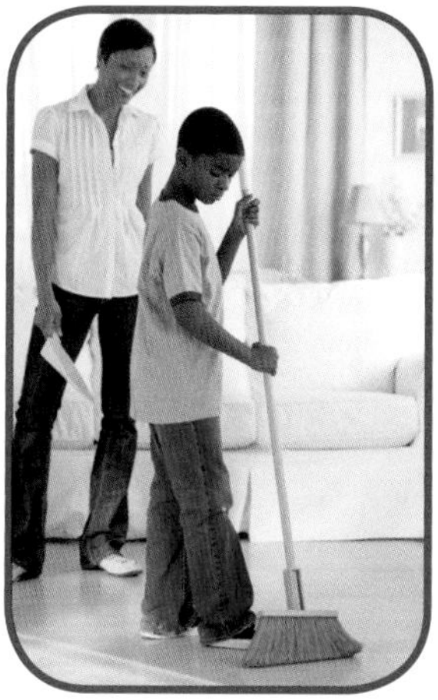

2.

3.

Words with ea, ie

Look at each picture. Read the words.

Example:

seal

leaf

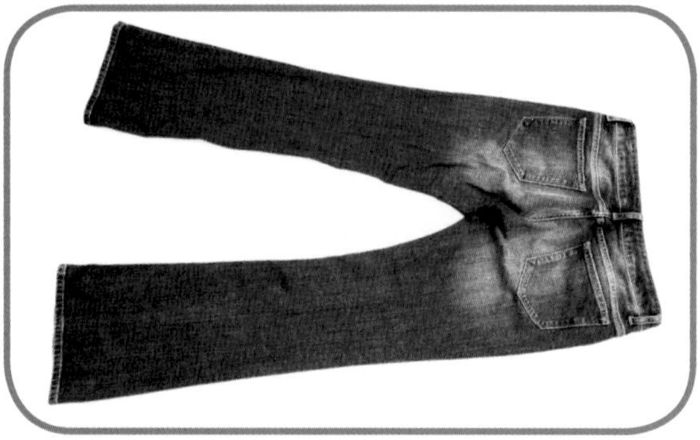

jeans

chief

field

windshield

Key Words

Read the sentences. Match each sentence to one or more pictures.

High Frequency Words

- been
- both
- different
- friend
- great
- house
- kind
- place

Helping in Different Ways

1. People help each other in **different** ways.
2. A **friend** can help you **both** work and play.
3. You can find helpers all over the **place**.
4. A teacher is one **kind** of helper.
5. A teacher teaches you **great** things.
6. Have you **been** a helper in your **house**?

What are some different ways to help?

Phonics Games
NGReach.com

Real Helpers

by Ana Gonzalez

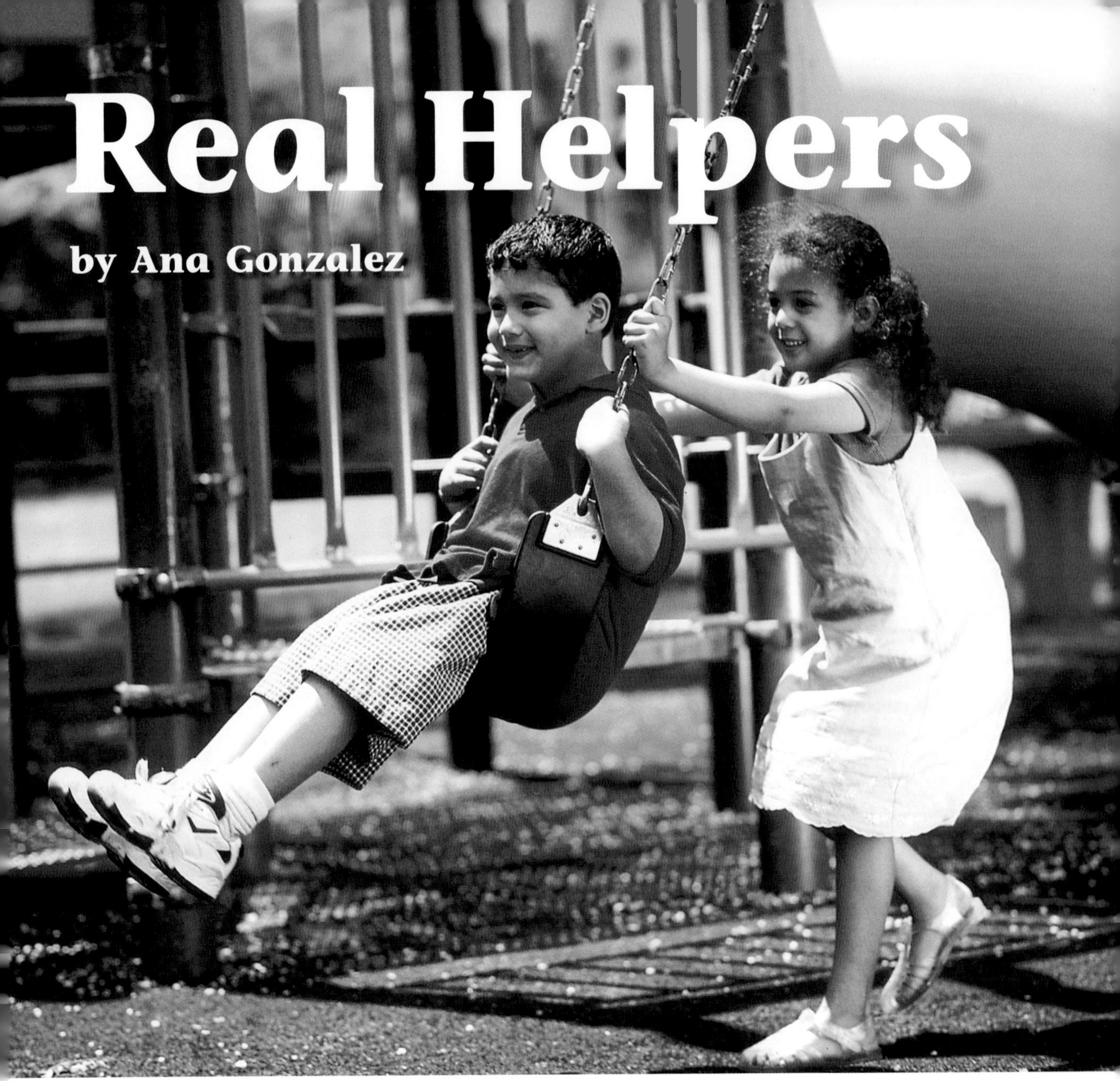

People help each other in different ways. A friend can help you feel glad.

People help us with the work they do, too. Look at these people. They both have important jobs. But if you get a disease or feel weak, who will heal you?

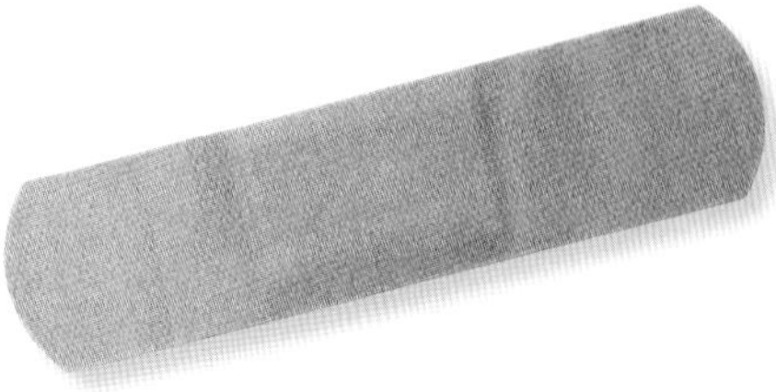

A doctor heals people. If you have a cut, a doctor will clean it. She can rub cream on it to help it heal. She can treat the sick.

Both of these people do important jobs. But when you need to eat a meal, who will you go see?

A farmer is the one to see! A farmer raises crops for us to eat. A farmer plants wheat and peanuts in his fields. A farmer plants peaches and beans.

If a drain in your house leaks or gets clogged, who can help? What will he do?

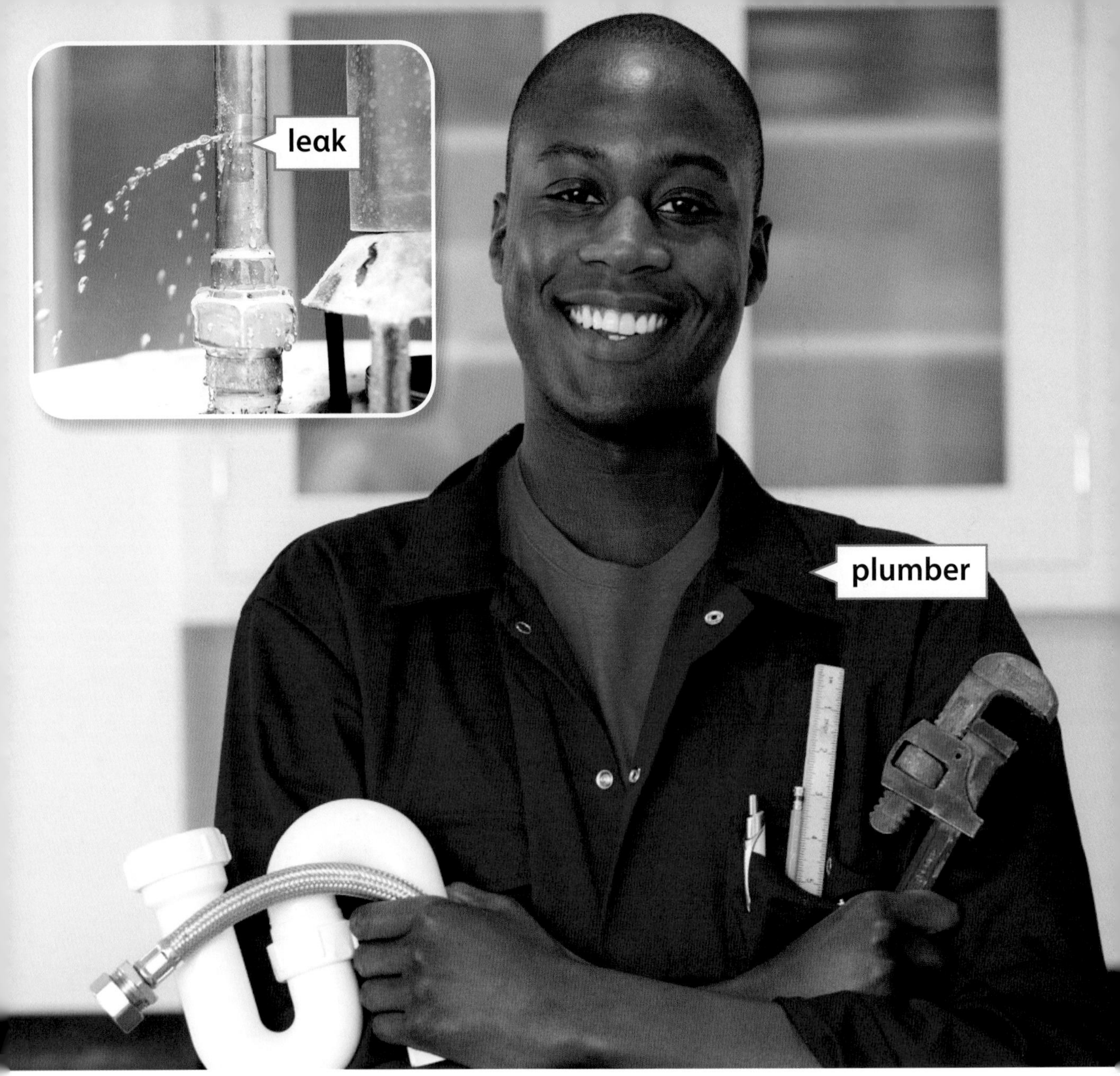

This man can stop a leak. He is a plumber. His job is to seal leaking pipes. This is important! You don't want a pipe to send a stream of water all over your house.

We need both of these people at different times. They both have important jobs. But who will teach you to read?

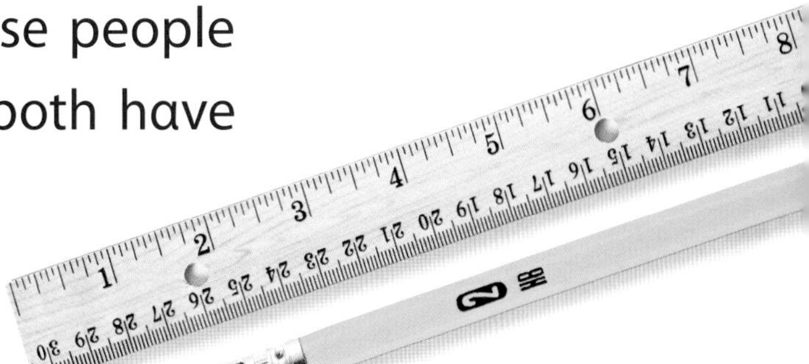

Teachers can teach different things. One teacher may teach you to read. A different teacher may teach you to swim or to make a meal.

Both of these people do important work. You can ask one of them to look up a fact. But the other one helps to keep the public safe. Who is it?

The police keep us safe. They may stop a thief or rescue a pet. They are great friends!

Lots of people help us. Who do you help? ❖

Words with **ea, ie**

Read these words.

read	chief	raise	field	fix
leaks	thief	treats	peaches	make

Find the words with **ea** or **ie**.
Use letters to build them.

r e a d

Talk Together

Choose words from the box above to tell your partner what each man can do to help.

The man can fix leaks for us.

1.

2.

3.

Crossword Puzzle

Across

1 This street has one on it. We'd like to be there.

4 Green beans and red beans are _____ colors.

6 sweet treats that'll grow on trees

8 Have you ever _____ a real helper?

Down

2 kind of place you plant a seed

3 These are people who teach you to read. They've been a big help.

5 A plumber can fix _____ a clog and a leaking pipe.

7 Your best friend is _____ .

Words to Use

both	peaches	field	house
been	teachers	great	different

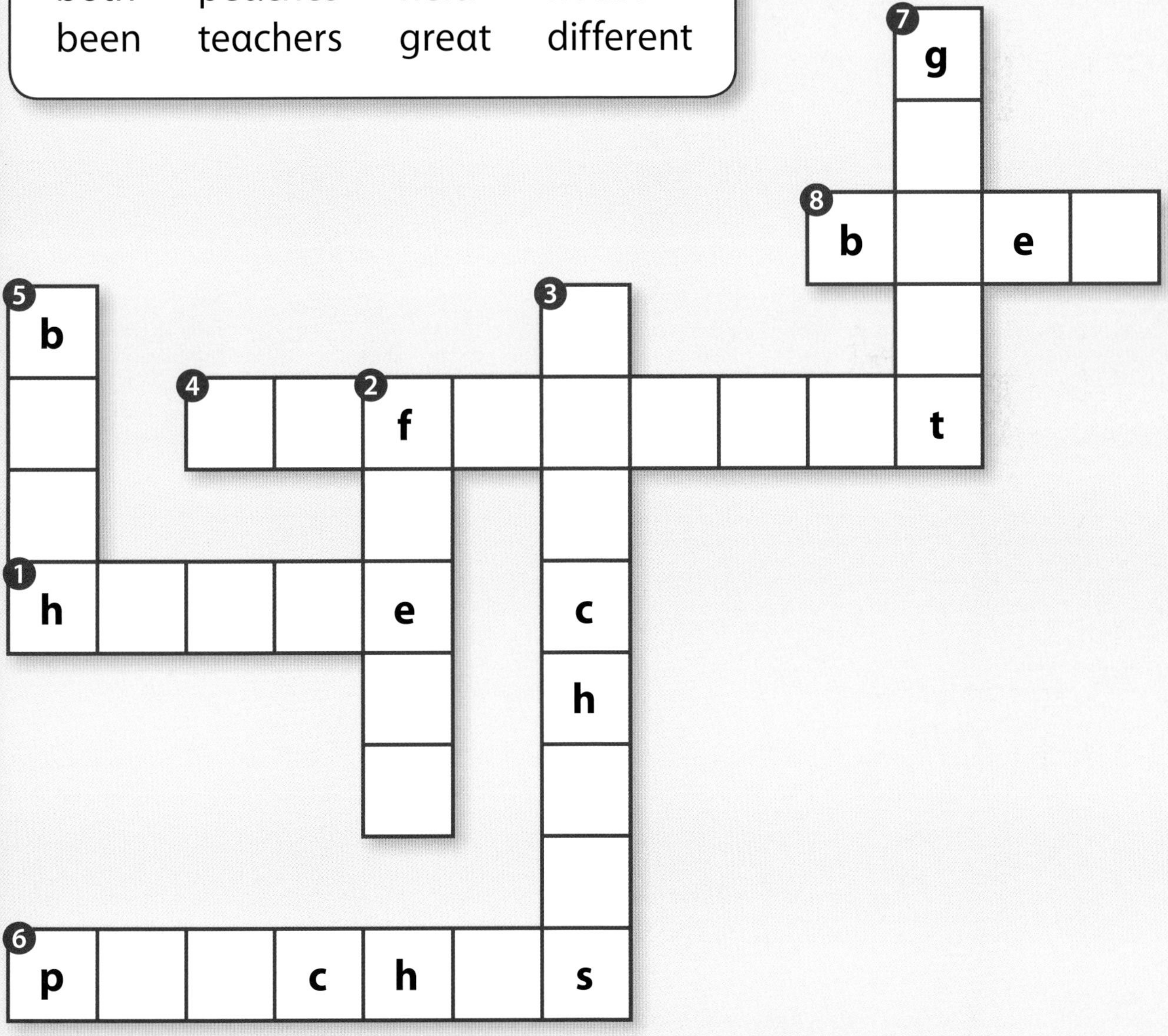

Acknowledgments
Grateful acknowledgment is given to the authors, artists, photographers, museums, publishers, and agents for permission to reprint copyrighted material. Every effort has been made to secure the appropriate permission. If any omissions have been made or if corrections are required, please contact the Publisher.

Photographic Credits
CVR Comstock/Getty Images. **2** (bl) Jill Lang/Shutterstock. (cl) Creatas/Jupiterimages. (rcb) Alexander Walter/Digital Vision/Getty Images. (rct) G.K. & Vikki Hart/Photodisc/Getty Images. (tl) David Levinson/Corbis. **3** Liz Garza Williams/Hampton-Brown/National Geographic School Publishing. **15** (br) Mia Song/Star Ledger/Corbis. (c) Eri Morita/Getty Images. (l) JGI/Tom Grill/Getty Images. (tr) Liz Garza Williams/Hampton-Brown/National Geographic School Publishing. **16** (bl) Bruce Rolff/Shutterstock. (br) Artville. (cl) Elnur/Shutterstock. (rcb) Gaetano/Corbis. (rct) DigitalStock/Corbis. (tl) Corel. **17** (bc) Liz Garza Williams/Hampton-Brown/National Geographic School Publishing. (l) Jupiterimages. (r) GeoM/Shutterstock. (tc) Monkey Business Images/Shutterstock. **18** Richard Hutchings/PhotoEdit. **19** (b) PhotoDisc/Getty Images. (l) Getty Images. (r) Olga Vasilkova/Shutterstock. **20** Getty Images. **21** (b) Artville. (l) TanyConstantine/Corbis Premium RF/Alamy Images. (r) Michael Krinke/iStockphoto. **22** Michael Krinke/iStockphoto. **23** (b) YinYang/iStockphoto. (l) Concettina D'Agnese/Shutterstock. (r) Juice Images/Alamy Images. **24** (bg) Juice Images/Alamy Images. (inset) DIGIcal/iStockphoto. **25** (br) Sean Locke/iStockphoto. (l) PhotoDisc/Getty Images. (tr) Jeffrey Smith/iStockphoto. 26 PhotoDisc/Getty Images. **27** (b) Klaus Sailer/iStockphoto. (l) David Hiller/PhotoDisc/Getty Images. (r) Jupiterimages/Comstock Images/Alamy. **28** David Hiller/PhotoDisc/Getty Images. **29** Liz Garza Williams/Hampton-Brown/National Geographic School Publishing.

Illustrator Credits
3, 29 Nancy Carlson; **4-14** Valeria Cis; **30** Jannie Ho

National Geographic School Publishing
Hampton-Brown
www.NGSP.com

Printed in the USA.
Quad Graphics, Leominster, MA

ISBN:978-0-7362-8069-3

17 18 19
10 9 8 7 6